Taking Care of Myself

Trying Hard in School

By Meg Gaertner

level 2 little blue readers

www.littlebluehousebooks.com

Little Blue House is distributed by North Star Editions:
sales@northstareditions.com | 888-417-0195

Produced for Little Blue House by Red Line Editorial.

Photographs ©: Shutterstock Images, cover, 4, 11, 13, 14–15, 16, 19, 21, 22–23, 24 (top left), 24 (top right), 24 (bottom left), 24 (bottom right); iStockphoto, 6, 9

Library of Congress Control Number: 2021916797

ISBN
978-1-64619-497-1 (hardcover)
978-1-64619-524-4 (paperback)
978-1-64619-575-6 (ebook pdf)
978-1-64619-551-0 (hosted ebook)

Printed in the United States of America
Mankato, MN
012022

About the Author

Meg Gaertner enjoys reading, writing, dancing, and being outside. She lives in Minnesota.

Table of Contents

Trying Hard

Trying hard in school helps people learn.

Everyone learns differently.

But certain skills help people be more successful at school.

At Home

Being organized is a skill.
Being organized means
having the things you need.
It also means knowing where
to find those things.

School supplies might include notebooks, colored pencils, and more. Keep your school supplies together in one place. That way, you will always know where to find what you need.

notebook
colored pencils

Spend time
each afternoon
doing homework.
Find a quiet place if
possible, and turn off
the TV.
Gather the supplies
you need.
Then do your homework,
and check it for mistakes.

Study a little bit every day. That way, you will feel prepared for school. Ask your teacher for tips on how to study.

Pack your backpack each night before bed. Put your school supplies in the backpack. That way, you will be ready in the morning.

backpack

desk

At School

Pay attention in class, and listen closely to your teacher. Work quietly at your desk. Ask questions if you do not understand something.

Maybe you have a hard time paying attention. If so, talk to your teacher. He or she can find ways to help.

2 + 4 = 8
2 + 5 = 10

Sometimes your teacher will ask questions. Raise your hand to answer them. Speak only when your teacher calls on you.

hand

You might give a wrong answer sometimes, but that's okay.
Making mistakes is part of learning.
Your teacher will help you find the right answer.

teacher
live out people
who work
6. bike
7. dime
8. hide
9. ice
10. kite
use

Glossary

backpack

desk

colored pencils

notebook

Index